Sir George Douglas

Poems of a Country Gentleman

Sir George Douglas

Poems of a Country Gentleman

ISBN/EAN: 9783744713252

Printed in Europe, USA, Canada, Australia, Japan

Cover: Foto ©Thomas Meinert / pixelio.de

More available books at **www.hansebooks.com**

POEMS

OF A

COUNTRY GENTLEMAN

BY

SIR GEORGE DOUGLAS, BART.

AUTHOR OF 'THE FIRESIDE TRAGEDY'

'Dolgomi ancor che non ho conosciuto
  La giovanezza, e il bel tempo che ho avuto,
  Se non or quando egli è in tutto perduto!'

LONGMANS, GREEN, AND CO.
39 PATERNOSTER ROW, LONDON
NEW YORK AND BOMBAY
1897

All rights reserved

DEDICATION

Bow'd, with self-mistrusting fears,
After thrice a hundred years,
Shade of Beaumont! One who loves
Thy fountain-heads, thy pathless groves—
One who, averse from noise and folly,
With thee had woo'd sweet Melancholy
(Ah! that who so fondly loved
More constant in his suit had proved!)—
Here where the stone records thy death,
Here I hang this funeral wreath!

Twining this I pass'd unheeding
Myrtle, rose, and love-lies-bleeding.
Passion-flower, or eglantine,
May lure the lover's hand, not mine:
I pass'd onward, seeking rather
Wilding growths and rank to gather,
(Sweet—if those be sweet which bloom
Round the Remorseful Poet's tomb),—
Poppy or hop-wreath to unite
With the wan flowerets of the night!

Such thy grave I now strew on—
Alms for austere Oblivion!

CONTENTS

	PAGE
DEDICATION	v

POEMS OF NATURE AND SOLITUDE

SPRING, SONG, AND SOLITUDE	3
A NIGHT-PIECE	5
THE TRUMPET	11
THE OMEN	12
TOADSTOOLS: A FANCY	14
THE MORALIST IN AUTUMN	16
THE 'LIGHTNING BEFORE DEATH'	18
THE WANING YEAR	19
PRESENTIMENT	20
FRAGMENT OF A REVERIE	21
WINTER EXILE IN THE SOUTH	26
THE NURSE'S TALE	27
THE ANTIQUITY OF ART	40
'THE PONY'S WELL'	42
'ON THE ROMAN WALL'	44
ELEGY ON AN ANGLER-POET	46

CONTENTS

SONGS AND POEMS

	PAGE
A Winter Song	53
Three Songs	54
Song	56
Evening: an Eclogue	57
'Hide and Seek'	60
A Last Farewell	62
A Love-missive	63
'La Morte Amoureuse'	64
ΠΡΟΠΕΜΠΤΙΚΟΝ	66
For the Last Night of the Year	68
A Sibylline Leaf	69
Gratitude	70
Death and Life	72
Notes	73

POEMS OF NATURE AND SOLITUDE

'Moods of fantastic sadness, nothing worth'

SPRING, SONG, AND SOLITUDE

I

The Spring returns : the Earth grows young—
  Grows young as never man shall grow—
And cries, with many a silvery tongue,
  As loud and clear as long ago.

The world is green : in every vein
  New life with new-born gladness thrills :
The light of Youth is found again !
  Hear and rejoice, ye patriarch hills !

II

The woodland bird, when Spring returns,
  Pours all its gladness on the air ;
And sings the joys the loved one earns—
  Sings that the earth is green and fair :

And would that I, like thee, sweet bird,
   Might set my joys, my sadness free,
Singing—uncared for and unheard—
   A song that's all too hard for me!

III

Oh, in this fair far-off retreat,
   At patient Evening's peaceful hour,
As our first father met, to meet—
   Where shades are deep, in brake or bower—

Some form of female loveliness,
   As white as if a moonbeam fell—
Come from another world to bless,
   And evermore with me to dwell!

A NIGHT-PIECE

When saner men are sound a-bed,
    And beasts in woods and fields are still,
The lonely paths alone I tread,
    And wander on o'er dale and hill :

O'er waste and woodland, ford and fence
    My onward course uncheck'd I steer,
Unseen—as walks the Pestilence,
    When damps infect the sorrowing year.

The screech-owl from her touchwood house
    Peeps forth, and chides me as I go,
That thus her fretful chicks I rouse
    And through the echoing woods halloo.

For no latch clicks ; no footstep beats
    In tune to mine the loud highway,
Save his, whose face the night secretes—
    Whose craft abhors the eyes of day.

What goal have I to gain to-night?
    Yon haunted tower, or yonder hill,
Which, on the utmost verge of sight,
    Cuts clear into the twilight still?

Not these: a friendlier bourn I know,
    Five furlongs from the neighbouring town,
Where, o'er the broad champaign below,
    A bench-encircled beech looks down:—

A pleasant haunt when eves are long,
    And mild, and full of balm, in May;
When wordy elders round it throng,
    And children with the beech-mast play;

And lovers, lingering on till night—
    Still whispering with the still-whispering leaves—
Score on its bark the troth they plight,
    And many a trust the tree receives:

A pleasant spot when ponderers see
    The sweet old tale retold once more,
Mature Content and infant Glee—
    The simple life-play acted o'er.

A NIGHT-PIECE

But now—when Life is laid to sleep,
    And its unlantern'd watchman I ;
Who hear alone the wheezing sheep,
    And, far away, the wild-duck's cry—

Now smile with more congenial air
    Forsaken seat and sombre tree ;
Which smiled, with light and laughter there,
    For all the world, but not for me.

This hour is mine :—on couch or straw,
    The scheming active myriads lie—
Clownish contempt with kingly awe,
    Like garments for the time laid by.

Oh, then, that pains of pride and power
    Might with the drear night pass away !
And brothers in the midnight hour
    Arise to brotherhood with day !

This hour is mine. A charmer's hands,
    The finger'd branches o'er me pass ;
Whilst, rustling, in the woods expands
    The Spring's new life in leaves and grass ;

Till Sleep, from dreamland's confines pale—
  That lazy lover of soft sound—
Floats on the hawthorn-incensed gale,
  And weighs me, nerveless, to the ground;

With silk-smooth arms about my neck,
  And cozening whispers in my ear—
As idle as the chattering beck,
  Which none but dreamers pause to hear;—

Till, as from some insidious cup,
  Inspired forbidden powers to wield,
Strange phantoms could I conjure up
  To move and mime in yon grey field.

Behold! the shades of all those lives
  That fill'd the evening air with noise—
Grave husbands with their mild-faced wives,
  And grandsires crook'd, and girls and boys;

Striplings and maidens, hand in hand,
  And babes—our life's small sweet spring flowers,—
Like strangers—in a far-off land
  Mindful of home and bygone hours—

A NIGHT-PIECE

Come back once more;—and, one by one,
    With wistful mien and eyes downcast—
Weak wraiths from worlds without a sun—
    Still silently go trooping past.

So sad to see I scarce can stay
    For 'By your leave,' or, 'With your leave,'
To take my stand beside the way
    And pluck the foremost by the sleeve.

'Now, gossip, whither, pray, so late?—
    Hark! though the noon of night be near,
Dawn yet shall burst his dungeon-gate—
    Where Doubt stands sentinel with Fear—

'And, o'er old Ocean's labouring waste,
    O'er silent city, stretching plain,
Charged with dear hope, enjoin'd to haste,
    Shall ride, a messenger, amain—

'An angel—and like angels bright,
    Arm'd with the name that all revere,
Who hark, and speed him on his flight
    To find and greet and help us here!

'When he, from yonder glimmering slope,
    Pausing his outworn steed to breathe,
Waves his plumed casque, and shouts us, "Hope!"
    Hope to the hearts that touch on death!

'Then straight, from signal-tower and hill,
    Our watchmen shall give on the cry;
Which, through the throng'd streets echoing still,
    Shall reach the hearts that faint and die;—

'Till, with one voice, around, afar,
    Tongued like the forests, winds and waves,
Choir upon choir shall hail the Star—
    The Morning Star that speaks and saves!'

So, in the enthusiasm of my sleep,
    Moved by strong love and pity, I spake;
When, pierced with words like flames that leap,
    I started from the ground awake!

I stood alone.—That sorrowing train
    O'er the bleak world had ta'en its way—
Ne'er on my sight to rise again,
    Though life be blest with many a day.

THE TRUMPET

I PACED a path 'neath tall green trees,
   Whose few steep branches met on high,
At the sad hour when, by degrees,
   The light fades in the dull grey sky;

When, somewhere—oh! I know not where—
   Like sunlight broken on Night and Fear—
A voice of joy amidst despair—
   Sounded a trumpet loud and clear!

Then—with that strong o'ermastering cry—
   From burden'd brows and breast in pain,
Rush'd to these eyelids long gone dry
   Tears! with a touch set free, like rain.

THE OMEN

The face of Day was strange ; it seem'd malign :
    The Sun, like Fortune that showers gold on men,
Nor on the morn, nor all thro' noon did shine—
    Averted—as tho' ne'er to turn again !

Alone and lonely, in my lonesome room,
    (My eyes were heavy, but my heart was lead)
From morn till eve, still seated in the gloom,
    Idle, with listless hands, I had hung my head.

At length I rose,—beset with many fears
    And fancies bad ;—a grandsire at four-score,
Bearing the burden of his sins and years,
    Had dragg'd his limbs as nimbly to the door.

Vast clouds o'erspread the heaven : the air was hush ;
    Until a whisper stirr'd the dark green leaves
(As I stood listening there) on tree and bush—
    Like Conscience when she cannot rest and grieves.

THE OMEN

I raised my eyes, and saw where, thro' the sky—
    Coursers of joy, with lustrous necks extent—
Two wild-ducks, straining, side by side did fly—
    To some far nest, their home, ere nightfall bent.

Then straight—like Remus, watching from his hill
    The flights of birds—I, shuddering, call'd aloud :
'What omen . . . ?   In the abyss of unknown hill,
    Tell me what secrets do the years enshroud ?'

TOADSTOOLS: A FANCY

Now Autumn spreads the fall-cloud o'er the field,
    Ere eventide is come;
Now a swift growth old woods and pastures yield,
    Whilst all is dark and dumb,—
Fair wholesome mushrooms, sought by girls at dawn,
    On meadows thick with dew;
And, strewn like writing on smooth verge and lawn,
    The noisome fungus too.

    Nature has aspects infinite;
        And Man has that within,
    May think it reads her meanings right
        With fancies gross from sin.

And so, erewhile, when issuing from my door—
    The Adam of a new-created Earth—
The toadstool-group a hideous aspect wore,
    By yon tree-roots—last night's portentous birth.

TOADSTOOLS : A FANCY

For swarming thick, like snake-heads those appear'd,
   With leprous scales, like an ill-liver's skin,
Bloody from shambles, poison-rank, and weird
   With malice, mischief, mockery from within !

Kind Nature ! shield me from like thoughts with these ;
   And grant me more to know
Your saving health, your temperance, and peace, —
   Point me the way to go.
I would be firm and constant, pure and kind ;
   Loving, but wisely, not amiss ;
Ruling rash thoughts with Heaven-directed mind :
   Dear Nature, teach me this !

THE MORALIST IN AUTUMN

These autumn morns are bright and fair . . .
Behold the fairy flashing there
Of the new-spun gossamer !
And on this dewy greensward trace
The broken ring—the halting-place
Where fairies, in their whirling flight,
The tenth part of a moment light . . .
And lo ! by waste and woodland on,
To other moonlit games are gone !

I heard the tale of a rustic wight,
Who, passing on his ways by night,
Had chanced, an instant, in amaze,
On the fairy-folk to gaze.
With him, his simple neighbours tell
How nothing from that hour went well.
His hand its whilome art forgot ;
He droop'd—he pined for what was not :

THE MORALIST IN AUTUMN

His spirit stray'd—like one who strays
From old, endear'd, accustom'd ways;
And, pale and lonesome, like a ghost,
For ever seeking something lost,
From human warmth and kin estranged
He wander'd, isolated, changed.

I, even I, am such as he
Since erst, divinest Poesy!
Upon my soul, upon my sight,
Dawn'd thy too radiant morning-light.
I would I knew a fairy spell
To heal the heart and make all well!

'THE LIGHTNING BEFORE DEATH'

'Tis Autumn. . . . How the world is hush'd !
    Does it forebode the end ?
    Never ! for every tree and plant
    Wears motley, gay—extravagant—
Such as the hopeful, young, all-conquering Spring,
    Array'd in tenderest green,
Dame Nature's darling, grudged not anything,
    Hath neither dream'd nor seen !

    Yet, even as now
    The world of lifeless things grows fair,
    Setting the crown of beauty on its brow,
    In the hush'd autumnal air :
So I, when watching by the bed of death,
    Have known the clouded mind grow clear,
Have miss'd the trouble from the vexèd breath,
    And said, The end is near !

THE WANING YEAR

WITH faded leaves her path was strown—
   Gold of the elm and beechen red :
She wander'd—she was all alone—
   The Summer and her hopes were dead.

She murmur'd—for her pulse beat low,
   'Oh, we were glad in spring-time here !
Who would have thought it ended so ?'
   She murmur'd . . . and let fall a tear.

'The air is full of voices faint ;
   The rain is cold and dim the day :
No ear gives heed to my complaint—
   'Tis time I were away !'

PRESENTIMENT

'Tis winter and the skies are dull,
    The snow is softly falling:
My hope is dead, my heart is full;
    The Past is past recalling:

A lonely bird sings clear and free
    'Neath yon deep arch of boughs;
Her song is this—reproach to me,
    Woe to my father's house!

FRAGMENT OF A REVERIE

Cool in the shadow of a cloud
   That slowly cross'd the mountain-side
I sat, and thought my thoughts aloud,
   And mused on life's advancing tide.

Around me stretch'd those fields of stone
   That hood the toilworn Pilgrim grey
Who guards, eternally alone,
   The softly blue Sicilian bay :

And down from coign and rock-bound height
   The numerous-handed prickly-pear
Glared, wan with hard excess of light—
   It seem'd a guardian dragon there :—

Whilst, round me, scatter'd boulder-stones—
   Dwarves in the grey-beards' council met,
With pain who shift their senile bones—
   Rose in a narrower circle set :

Such shapes of Eld, so fateful-still,
    The lizards—offspring of the Sun,
Who from fire-fountains feed their fill—
    About their ankles fearless run.

Thus couch'd, I mused on Youth's decline,
    On Aspiration still proved vain ;
And told the seasons conquer'd mine,
    And the sad seasons lost to Pain.

And, o'er the landscape of the Past,
    I saw my faltering footsteps traced,
As o'er a scene where Night falls fast
    And stormful on a weary waste.

But, as when Night with storms descends
    In darkness on the wind-swept plain,
Some parting shafts the day-star sends
    To pierce the watery heav'ns again—

So, 'mid suspense and gloom profound,
    Some scatter'd sun-gleams, here and there
Caught from the threatening skies around
    A light of radiance heavenly-fair !

And pondering where these joy-beams fell
   (Like isles of hope in barbarous seas,
Where mild and civil nations dwell,
   In husbandry and arts of peace)—

Whether where troops of tedious men
   Judge at their ease the things which be,
And Wit and Lightness vex again
   The soul of sad Sincerity;

Or on yon flint-strewn path which leads
   To lonely Lore's austere renown;
Or else where Love with rose-thorns bleeds,
   And drags the aspiring angel down . . .

'O never there mine hours of joy,
   Health and heart-quickening hope for men;
But now, in childhood, as a boy,
   When thou wert with me, Nature, then!'

I spake; and—as from bonds and night
   Forth-issuing on the bounteous air,
On the free earth and generous light—
   Stretch'd out my hands toward heav'n in pray'r.

' O Nature, Mother—thou who erst
    Fostered'st my thoughtless infant hours,
From springs of beauty fed, and nursed
    'Midst woods and waters, fields and flowers—

' O Mother, claim thy wandering son !
    The years deal hardly by me—yet,
Tho' friends forget me one by one,
    And leave me, thou wilt not forget.

' For oh ! tho' changed, tho' fall'n I be,
    Since, like the new Spring's tenderest lamb,
Sportful and pure I play'd by thee,
    The world has made me all I am !

' This was that loving, love-lapp'd child,
    Who, nestling to thy all·nurturing breast,
Draughts of a virtue undefiled
    Suck'd, and caress'd and was caress'd :

' This was that little lonely boy,
    Who, when his school-room task was done,
Turn'd to thee with the returning joy
    Of husbands in the espousèd one !

'Dost thou not know me . . . ? Oh that then
  Some rough stream hurrying to the sea
(With whom my weak limbs fought in vain)
  Had spied me, and laid hold on me;

'And, fretting ever and anon,
  Quiet cheek or irresponsive hand,
In his rude play, had borne me on
  To tides and bars and the sea-sand!

'Would that thy lightning, from some cloud
  Swoll'n to fantastic shapes of doom,
Had touch'd and, from the shuddering crowd,
  Had beckon'd me to th' unyielding tomb!

.   .   .   .   .   .

WINTER EXILE IN THE SOUTH

O ALIEN flowers ! unseasonable blooms,
    That, in this new translucent, temperate air,
Hide the sad truth, like garlands hung from tombs !
    Winter within makes winter everywhere :
And nothing me your specious splendours stead,
    Your aloes' scarlet, your magnolia's snow ;
That, strange to that far clime where I was bred,
    Speak not of home and friends and long ago.

THE NURSE'S TALE

If that be truth which once would scare
Yeoman and hind and villager
On nightly errands bound—poor souls !
And send 'em skurrying to their goals,
Breathless, with unreverted eye,
Beside themselves they knew not why,—
If it be truth that restless sprites
Seek their old earthly haunts o' nights—
As, misers for their buried gold
Their hiding-places never told ;
The lady treacherously foredone
There where she met her trysted one
(By the half-filled pits to this day
She wails and wrings her hands, they say),—
If it be sooth that dead men roam,
My ghost for sure will haunt my home !

Then past my date, despite mine heir,
My old abode I still shall share ;
And so these scenes I daily roved—
Scenes beautiful and well-beloved—

These gardens, shrubberies, woods shall gain
A poetry of half-human strain;
Such that when stirs on summer eves
The light wind in the whispering leaves,
If any dreamer chance to hear,
Alert, nor wholly free from fear,
He'll fancy in the prolong'd still tone
A mystic meaning all its own.

Then haply One—on whose young life,
Her gifts with bale and blessing rife
Largely th' unequal muse has shed—
Pillowing at eve his golden head
(Her darling) on his nurse's knee
Shall beg with sly cajolery,
Sweet coaxing, artful threats of tears,
The food his fancy craves yet fears.
(This when the hand that now with joy
Guides the swift pen, and speeds the ploy,
Dust with my fathers' dust laid low,
Is gone the way all flesh must go!)

Then may the Dame reluctant yield,
Her inward pride but ill conceal'd,
And from her lips, in tones grown weak,
The voice of bygone days shall speak.

THE TALE

ONCE on a time—nay, who knows when?
Yet once—if there be truth in men,
In yon fine house, half-hidd'n in trees,
That in his walks my honey sees,
As laird, tho' passing poor, did dwell
A man of whom strange tales they tell!
No ill he wrought, save—as 'tis said—
To nurse strange fancies in his head
(Poor trash these fancies, such as can
Nor fill a beast nor feed a man!)
Yet, so the whimsies in him wrought,
He grew, as one might say, distraught.
Poor gentleman! sad fortune his,
(He could not help himself, I wis);
Yet, by my life! his case was hard,
From sport and business both debarr'd!
For, sauntering with some musty book,
His pleasure lonesomely he took;

And sat to canvass grave affairs
Like one who neither hears nor cares;
Till, pounds and pence regarding not,
God's blessèd world seem'd quite forgot!

Then as in some queer world, they tell,
Of his own fashioning would he dwell.
Then, night by night, his casement shone —
Like some small star that gleams alone—
Whilst, in most vain yet arduous toil,
He sate to burn the midnight oil,—
Content without reward to pore
On tomes of crabb'd and tedious lore,
Or knit th' unprofitable rhyme,
Whilst growing poorer all the time!
(How much such feckless labour steads
Is plain to all but addleheads!)

Then on the highways would he rove,
Like one bewitch'd, or cross'd in love,
With wild and interrupted pace —
Now stopping short, as if to trace
Lost footprints in the dust; anon,
As having found them, hastening on.
Or, by the wayside, on the grass,
Idle he'd sit to watch folk pass,

THE TALE

Staring—yet with an eye so dim
He saw not half of who saw him.
Or, with none by, he'd speak aloud,
Yet seem as new-fall'n from a cloud
If any words with him would change ;
And when he spoke his speech was strange.

A faded leaf, or wayside flower,
Served him for pastime for an hour :
Dearly he prized the scentless rose
That thick on every hedgerow blows ;
Blue speedwell, or the pale harebell,
He'd pluck as though he loved them well,
And on their leaves and petals small
(This was his oddest freak of all),
Like one consoled for griefs and fears,
Gaze, as with rapture, or with tears !

Yet most by night he loved to roam
The fields and woods around his home ;
Or, spectre-like, to stalk abroad
On some deserted country road.
Alas, poor heart ! He wrought none ill.
Our worst afflictions are God's will !
Long since he to his rest is gone,
Where wise and simple are as one ;

Long since, beside his kindred laid,
He slumbers by the yew-tree shade :
Hard by, the murmuring waters roll,
But wake him not : God rest his soul !

And yet, if truth the gossips tell,
His soul rests but indifferent well.
Not I this story's truth attest—
I had it at third-hand at best ;
I only know that candidly
I tell you what was told to me !

Hob Hobnail was a precious lad,
For him no ploy was e'er too bad ;
A tippler, poacher, roysterer bold,
His misdeeds cannot half be told !
Well ! 'twas this graceless creature's way
To skulk in taverns half the day,
Till, waxing valiant after dark,
He'd scale the fence and cross the park,
To spread his nets, or watch his snares—
A foe to partridges and hares.

One night, when faint the young moon shone,
Hob's comrade fail'd—he went alone.
All honest men were safe in bed :
The drink had mounted to his head.

THE TALE

Eerie, at times, it is and strange,
Methinks, in silent woods to range
Alone—with no companion near—
At noontide, tho' the sun shines clear.
But oh ! far eerier 'twere, I trow,
To thread the self-same woodland now.
For now the wanderer needs must stray
Reft of the comfort of the day ;
With small head now tuck'd 'neath its wing,
Sleeps every bird that blithe would sing ;
The happy harmless forest race,
The people of this desert place,
From shady aisle and verdant lawn
Are all, for some good cause, withdrawn ;
And 'twixt the trees and shadows mirk,
Who knows what hideous shapes may lurk ?
Yet, be his conscience only clear,
E'en now a man has nought to fear ;
But shadows, vapour, or the wind,
Suffice to scare a guilty mind !

Hob reach'd the pale, took heart of grace,
And stood within the glimmering chase,
Stifling the doubts within that grew
With visions of a savoury stew.

And now the fearsome woods are past,
The riverside is gain'd at last,—
Where broken elm and splinter'd saugh
Their nurture from the sandbanks draw;
Whilst, knee-deep, jungle-like, below
Hemlock and broad-leaved plantains grow.
With fever to his task address'd,
Hob winds his night-line with the best,—
Hauls his resisting spoil ashore,
And warms and chuckles at the splore!

But, hark! that sound unsure and low
That mingles with the river's flow—
Now rises high and almost clear,
Anon eludes the straining ear!
Not in dead Nature's power it lies—
The compass of her harmonies—
That faint yet ne'er mistaken noise,
The murmur of a human voice!
Stopp'd in his work, the startled clown
Plumps him amid the leafage down;
Where, hidden, with a single eye
He yet may scan the passer-by.

And nearer now, and yet more near,
He knows the object of his fear.

THE TALE

No keeper's this, or bailiff's tone !
This has an accent of its own,
Like some poor haverel in his lunes—
A voice that with itself communes.

With quaking heart, Hob bans the day,
And wishes himself miles away ;
For still the murmuring nears and nears :
He lists as with a thousand ears,
Nor, for his life, could steek his eye,
Altho' old Nick himself went by !

Not his that form, as shadow light,
That out of shadows comes in sight ;—
That form that with half-hidden face
Moves in such melancholy pace,
With eyes fix'd ever on the ground—
Still seeking something still not found ;
Which, moving, ever murmurs low
Of night, and fate, and long ago,
And—be it man, or be it wraith—
Descants on time, and life and death !

The trembling booby rubs his eyes :
On these he never more relies
If, o'er the misty river's brim,
Between the dying moon and him—

From his five senses well-nigh scared—
He has not recognised the Laird,
In likeness as he moved on earth—
A brother, of a different birth !

Why comes he here? on what strange job?
Hob doubts not but he comes for Hob—
Leaving his lodgings underground
On that most sorry errand bound !

Poor Hobnail's wit is clear and plain,
But what recks *he* of finer brain ?
What of the spirit's soaring wings—
Child of a day of little things ?
(Nor ours, if temper'd otherwise,
His clear discernment to despise.)
Yet, by my hope of heavenly bliss !
Man *has* a higher state than this.

Not as the slave of things that be,
Hemm'd in by dull utility,
Toward gain and sensual pleasure bent,
Apt to outwit or circumvent,
Commerce its element, its crown
Wealth and the honour wealth calls down,
To self and sordid interest wed—
Not thus our soul was fashionèd.

Confined within one narrow breast,
Like the caged lark, it will not rest,
But with vain efforts, wild desires,
Aching and agonised aspires.
Stifle and thwart it, still 'twill move,
Fluttering, its heavenly birth to prove;
And, drugg'd and poison'd, even in sleep
Murmurs complaint *not loud but deep!*
At common sights the tear will start,
And mortal things the immortal part
Will strangely touch—this truth was told
By Virgil, ere the world grew old.

Oh, then, some heaven of fancy give;
Some faith by which this soul may live!
A dream? Alas! Yet some high end—
One gave his life once for his friend:
If not towards gladness, let me rise
Towards heights of glad self-sacrifice—
This to the suppliant grant alone,
To feel for sorrows not his own!
For ring'd, encompass'd, hedged around
No outlet for his passion found,
Substance with spirit, both must die—
Life pass with immortality!

Of these our wants no Hobnail dreams;
To him a man is what he seems!
Not his 'neath surfaces to peer,
Enough for him the *now* and *here*.
But halt . . . *Quo tendis*, wayward elf?
The Nurse was speaking, not *myself*!
Resume the tale.—With one wild yell,
Hob flies as from the fiends of hell!

O'er park and pale long time he raced,
As tho' by fifty goblins chased;
And in a circle long he fled,
Stumbling, bogg'd, 'wilder'd and misled,
With streaming hair—so great his dread,
He fear'd, poor soul! to turn his head.
At length, bruised, batter'd, splash'd and torn,
By stone and stock, pool, mire, and thorn,
Fainting he fell, and falling knew
That tho' *he* fled, none did pursue.
Exhausted, homeward then he crept,
And said his prayers ere he slept;
And from that night, more cautious grown,
Respected what was not his own.

The tedious beldame's tale was told:
The fire burn'd low; sweet Five-years-old,

THE TALE

With eye fix'd on the speaker's face,
Not once had shifted in his place.
But now his bed-time long was past,
This tale, indeed, must be the last!
Sweetly he prays, with folded hands,
In words he hardly understands,
That God will keep him safe from sin—
Then lightly strips him to the skin,
And, by the little curtain'd bed,
Nurse pops the nightgown o'er his head,
And—as beside some rising stream—
Lays him to sleep, *perchance to dream*!

THE ANTIQUITY OF ART

(PALEOLITHIC MAN)

[Verses suggested by a stone axe-head discovered in a 'moss' in Teviotdale.]

A SAVAGE, in a bleak world, on a waste,
  'Midst fir-tree-cover'd mountains, led his life :
The claws and fangs of mighty beasts he faced—
  A hunter, seeking food for child and wife.

And, on the smooth wall of his cavern lair,
  The image of a reindeer once he drew,—
Small, to the life, with faithful lines and fair,
  That all its antlers' branchings copied true.

Was this a savage ? No ! a Man. The dew
  Of pity touch'd him ; the sweet brotherhood
Of Nature's general offspring well he knew :—
  Humane, he loved ; ingenious, understood.

More :—the desires that kindling hearts inflame
　　To leave dull rest, and court congenial woe—
The Love of Beauty, and the Thirst for Fame,
　　Throbb'd faintly in that huntsman long ago!

And, friend, the self-same passion in his breast
　　That stirr'd, and wrought to permanence divine
One form of grace, most touchingly express'd,
　　Stirs in your heart to-day, and stirs in mine!

'THE PONY'S WELL'

[Lines addressed to a Fountain in gratitude]

My thanks, kind fountain, for the fresh'ning draught,
    Wholesome and crystal-clear,
So oft by me, by my best-loved ones quaff'd,
    Thro' many a changing year!

For never, tho' the Sun with fieriest sheen
    Drank half the river dry,
Untimely sered the leaf, and scorch'd the green,
    Didst thou thy gift deny.

And—as unfailing—so without excess
    Dost thou thy bounty pour—
Yielding, regardless of the seasons' stress,
    Still neither less nor more.

'THE PONY'S WELL'

Thus as an infant, boldly, with stretch'd hand,
    Thy runlet would I prove,
Incredulous, and slow to understand
    That aught so quiet did move!

So, like some world-renouncing hermit old,
    To alms and temperance vow'd,
Unchanging, thou one equal course dost hold,
    Nor base, nor over-proud.

Green slopes surround, and tangled bushes gird,
    Thy moss-grown chamber small;
Above, the tall trees in the winds are stirr'd,
    And God is over all.

'ON THE ROMAN WALL'

[On the Roman Wall in Northumberland may be found a field-flower, (*Corydalis lutea*), one of the fumitories, which is a native of the Roman Campagna.]

   Fair, simply-blowing floweret wild,
    Small, short-lived star of earth,
   Thou, like some gipsy-stolen child,
    Art here of alien birth—

   (Here, where the grassy mound I trace,
    Green foss and ruin'd wall,
   That tells me of a conquering race
    And the proud conqueror's fall,)

   For, musing here on Hadrian's dyke,
    How far away seems Rome !
   And I, to find elsewhere thy like,
    Must seek it there, at home.

How camest thou thence? From that
    bright land
  March'd legions in array;
But whose the soft and gentle hand
    That brought the flower away?

Sick of the time and all its fears,
    Did some Italian maid,
Watering thee oft with secret tears,
    Nurse thee thro' shine and shade?

Yet—like the daughter of romance,
    Who in despite of fate
Raises the song and leads the dance,
    Beside a gipsy mate—

Thy bloom her scent and honey yields,
    And thou with spring dost blow—
A Roman flower in English fields—
    As bright as long ago!

Till, as one dreams, and idly thinks
    On wars and conquests vain,
A simple pastoral garland links
    Earth's mightiest nations twain.

ELEGY ON AN ANGLER-POET

By Tweed, by Teviot's winding tide,
    A form I knew is miss'd to-day!
The woods, the field, the rocks abide;
    But he has pass'd away—

Where, pensive—straying without an aim—
    As now, once more, these paths I trace
(Familiar haunts found still the same),
    I seek him in his place!

For seldom—(whether Tweed ran strong,
    Discolour'd, swoll'n with melting snows,
Awful with wrecks it bears along
    'Twixt banks it overflows;

Whether, with summer-shrunken stream—
    Where isles, before unknown, appear—
It sank in sloth, resign'd to dream)—
    I fail'd to meet him here!

Indeed—by drought, fair skies, or flood—
   So constant this his walk had been,
He seem'd, when met in fancy's mood,
   The Genius of the scene ;

Or, even—with venerable beard,
   In his right hand a willow rod—
Late sighted where his name was fear'd,
   The very river-god !

His date was from that Golden Age
   When, sprung from Hercules and Mirth,
In manhood and poetic rage,
   Giants still dwelt on earth.

In mountain, water, field, and wood,
   Their might was felt—empowered, at will,
The broods of earth, the sky, the flood,
   To capture, tame, or kill.

Then, by the fair lake's margent clear,
   What nights were theirs ! how brave a feast !
Ranged all in order, peer by peer,
   Where he was not the least.

Methinks the moon was full by night
  When Madness, madder than before,
Drank deep, and kept till broad daylight
  That table in a roar!

But envying Time, with marksman's art,
  Waging dire war, slew, one by one,
Their race, large-limb'd and light of heart—
  Till he remain'd alone:

And lingering, lonely, very old,
  Saw baser times, and knew instead
Men in whose veins the blood ran cold,
  With hearts where mirth was dead.

Yet still his peaceful craft he plied,
  Haunting by river, lake, and rill—
With power to common men denied,
  Assiduous, angling still,

Till all in wonderment cried out,
  When he, at eve, his ploy forsook—
From head to heel, and round about,
  Hung with the spoils he took!

ELEGY ON AN ANGLER-POET

He dipt his fingers in the flood
  (I heard an ancient angler tell),
And, nibbling, straight the finny brood
  Swarm'd at the charmer's spell.

And sometimes, too, with childlike glee,
  In praise of stream and riverside
He sang. A kindly man was he :
  And so, in time, he died.

And thus, by Teviot's rolling flood,
  His well-known form we miss to-day—
Gazing on river, field, and wood,
  Whence he has passed away !

Dear poet ! From that dead hand of thine,
  I (oh ! not rashly), born too late,
Claiming far kinship in the line,
  This legacy await :—

To others other gifts : to me,
  If I have praised thee here, at last,
Tho' ill, not unacceptably,
  Thy poet's pipe be pass'd !

Now, sleep ! Thy songs thou leavest with us :
Thy story be it our task to tell ;
But thee we now departing, thus,
Salute and bid 'Farewell !'

SONGS AND VERSES

A WINTER SONG

The wreath is faded from the reveller's brow,
    Never a flower remains !
Where is the beauty, where the gladness now,
    The lip the vintage stains ?

Fled as a dream !　But, by my dying fire,
    As I sit here alone—
The snowflakes spotting all her dusk attire,
    Enters a wrinkled crone :

' Cottage and hall alike must ope to me,'
    Says this unwelcome wife ;
' I come, uncall'd, to bear you company,
    And leave you but with life ! '

THREE SONGS

I

YESTERDAY

Could, oh could I, Yesterday!
   Of thy many moments one
Snatch and hide—and hie away,
   Like thieves who with their plunder run:

Over the far hills could I fly,
   Clasping it ever to my breast;
No Caliph were so rich as I,
   In Araby the Blest!

II

. A LOVE-SONG

Beloved, the world is ours to-night!
   Your fairness crowns you queen;
Whilst I am rich in such delight
   As seldom kings have seen:

THREE SONGS

And all I'd ask is utterance meet
   An after age to tell,
How life to one man once was sweet—
   How one heart once loved well!

III

WHITE VIOLETS

I planted violets o'er the grave
   Where sleeps my love alone :
No sweetness these pale flowerets have,
   No beauty like her own !

The longest winter's night must end :
   The Earth from death set free
Smiles and awakes—alas ! sweet friend,
   Comes there no Spring for me?

SONG

My soul escaped in music as in sleep
    The laggard body lay,
Bound, in a dungeon cavernous and deep . . .
    What cared the runaway?
Thro' the small grating, out into the night
    She pass'd, and took her flight.

Then o'er the summits of the forest old
    The happy madcap elf—
She whom no bounds in earth or heav'n should hold—
    Flew, singing to herself!
Ah! had she then known half she since has learn'd,
    She had ne'er, no ne'er, return'd!

EVENING: AN ECLOGUE

"Εσπερε, πάντα φέρεις, ὅσα φαινόλις ἐσκέδασ' αὔως,
φέρεις ὄϊν, φέρεις αἶγα, φέρεις ματέρι παῖδα.
SAPPHO'S Fragments.

First Shepherd—

    Now day draws to its close : the Sun
    Droops in the west, his journey done . . .

Second Shepherd—

    And, duly, from her mansion fair—
    Intent on charitable care—
    Bounteous, benign, of matchless worth,
    The gracious lady, Eve, comes forth;

First Shepherd—

    Upon whose head the kneeling clown
    Prays, as she goes, a blessing down.

Second Shepherd—

    Ay;—'tis her wish'd-for coming brings
    Sweet respite to all labouring things :

First Shepherd—

>'Tis she whose hand, with loving care,
>Lightens the burden all things bear . . .

Second Shepherd—

>And soothes each poor noon-fever'd brow—
>While murmuring comfort sweet and low—
>With gentle touch and cool.

First Shepherd—

>   'Tis she,
>Who, like a parent, tenderly—
>Gathering once more, as at the first,
>Whate'er the exuberant dawn dispers'd—
>By starlight, through the purple gloam,
>Leads all live things, her children, home !

Second Shepherd—

>She brings what, whilst the morn was grey,
>Heav'nward, with music, took its way,
>To range the air—with weary wings,
>The bird back to its nest she brings.

First Shepherd—

>Back to their fold she brings the flocks :

EVENING: AN ECLOGUE

Second Shepherd—

 Back from the field the toiling ox :

First Shepherd—

 Back to their caves all creatures wild :

Second Shepherd—

 Me back, once more, to wife and child !

First Shepherd—

 Dearer than morn, or night, or noon,
 To shepherd, Evening, is thy boon :

Second Shepherd—

 Than moon by night, or sun by day,
 Fairer, O Star of Eve, thy ray !

'HIDE AND SEEK'

[Reminiscence of Sorrow in Childhood.]

The old house is full of passages,
    With many a toilsome stair ;
I sought in those—I sought on these
    I could not find him there.

And room by room I wander'd through ;
    Each cupboard, corner, nook
I search'd, I ransack'd—high and low—
    Till I knew not where to look.

Then, in the garden, one long hour,
    I hunted everywhere :
The sweet-pea hedges were in flower—
    I peep'd . . . he was not there.

HIDE AND SEEK

Then I grew tired ; I call'd . . . In vain !
   From wall, and trees, and mound,
My own shout still came back again . . .
   He was not to be found !

The sun had sunk behind the hill ;
   The garden fill'd with shade ;
The turf with dew grew damp and chill ;
   At last I felt afraid.

With furtive glance I turn'd and fled—
   I reach'd my nursery warm ;
My nurse was there—she sooth'd my dread,
   And I was safe from harm :

But the hours pass'd heavily away ;
   For I could not forget.
I sought him many and many a day . . .
   But I have not found him yet.

And would that, in this world of grief,
   I knew—when all is past—
If then—oh, joy beyond belief !
   He shall be found at last.

A LAST FAREWELL

NATURE resumes her own to-night,
   And lets the tired-out poet sleep :—
Life's battle was too hard to fight,
   Life's mystery, to solve, too deep.
Grant him to rest ! he asks of death
   No more, who ask'd of life too much :
Heaven were to hear love's low-drawn breath
   Thro' dreams, and feel love's pitying touch.

A LOVE-MISSIVE

O, BEAUTY, kindness, purity,
    Are woman's noblest dower :
Rose-sweet, and not less fair is she,—
    Heav'n's star, earth's loveliest flower.
But, tho' no share in these you claim—
    You, who my heart possess—
I vow to love you all the same,
    And love you none the less !

For I will love for love's sweet sake,
    That can the world transform—
A garden in the desert make,
    A stillness 'midst the storm ;
That with one touch old bonds can break,
    And for old wrongs atone :
Then let me love for love's sweet sake,
    And that sweet sake alone !

'LA MORTE AMOUREUSE'

(FOR MUSIC)

As I lay dreaming, dreaming,
   By moonlight, o'er the dew
Came a form of fairest seeming—
   A form, a face, I knew.

My love stood by my side : she spake
   (As I lay dreaming),
'What dost thou here, beloved? Awake !'
   For I lay dreaming.

' Love, come away ! the night is serene,
The witches dance on the churchyard green,
The world is at rest, but ghosts are at play . . .
O love, I have sought thee ! O love, come away !'

'LA MORTE AMOUREUSE'

I rose from the ground and we mounted in haste,
We rode like the wind over mountain and waste !
O strange were the scenes that we pass'd in our ride,
But sweet were her words as she rode by my side !

We came to the hill-top with wild heaths around,
I heard in the distance the waterfall's sound,
And there, with my love, by the light of the moon,
With rapture I danced to a magical tune.

'O lost love, adieu !' 'O fair love, be true !'
We spake and we kiss'd 'mid the moonlight and dew . . .
Alas ! as we spake, with the dawning of day
My love, as I kiss'd her, pass'd softly away !

    And I lay dreaming, dreaming,
        By moonlight, 'midst the dew !
    That form of fairest seeming,
        That face no more I knew !

    But lonely, broken-hearted,
        And hopeless to forget
    How we met and kiss'd and parted,
        I am dreaming, dreaming yet !

ΠΡΟΠΕΜΠΤΙΚΟΝ

(CHRISTMAS EVE)

Go, little book!—ere morning's light
    You must be far upon your way—
A traveller, travelling post by night,
        Towards home and Christmas Day!

Go—and when daylight late shall break,
    When miles and miles are overflown,
When men to peace and gladness wake,
        Alight in London Town.

There, amid devious thoroughfares,
    Thro' mud and bustle, smoke and din,
Unerring, choose the path which bears
        Direct to Lincoln's Inn.

Seek the *Old Square*:—when that is found,
    The staircase number'd *Twenty-one*:
Gain the first landing from the ground—
        And, there, your journey's done!

ΠΡΟΠΕΜΠΤΙΚΟΝ

There dwells a man of judgment sound—
   Most polish'd, clear in speech, acute ;
Not plagued by dreams :—his Chambers found,
   Him, entering, salute.

And, from a friend than whose no heart
   For him with kindlier warmth can beat
(Boldly, with spirit, play your part)
   That Man of Parchments greet !

Whatever wish the Season brings—
   Luck, happiness, prosperity—
All good, all fair, all wished-for things—
   All these, wish him from me.

And tell him, if—to quote the saw—
   Wishes were steeds and clowns might ride,
I, not you, in the abode of Law,
   Should now be at his side !

Go, little book ! Yon eastern star
   Ere morning will have touch'd the west.
Go—travel safely, travelling far :
   Discharge a dear behest.

FOR THE LAST NIGHT OF THE YEAR

FRIENDS, as the stroke of twelve, alas !
    Booms from yon belfry-tower,
A soul, death-strick'n, toward Heaven shall pass,
    In his appointed hour :—

The Old Year—loth to take his flight
    In darkness, wind, and rain—
Shall bid the world a last 'good night,'
    Not to return again !

A SIBYLLINE LEAF

With time to manhood comes this truth :
  That not to taste, enjoy, attain ;
Not—as in dreams we nursed in youth—
  To love and to be loved again ;—
But to endure, self to control,
  To shape the void and fugitive,
Firm, with still upward-striving soul—
  This is to live and feel we live !

GRATITUDE

Oft I complain that these poor acts of mine—
  Light seeds sown broadcast in a barren field
    Wherein, beneath a lowering sky,
    The germ of life full soon must die—
  No harvest fair of love responsive yield :
    Oft I repine.

Would I no love to any creature bear,
  No act of kindness do,
    Except a guerdon be ensured
    For cherish'd love, or toil endured,
Richer, more beautiful and rare
  Than rubies of Peru ?
    (For such is Gratitude
    In a harsh world and rude !)

GRATITUDE

    No !
  Love is free,
  And scorns like usury.
  Let me then ask for nothing better
  Than to have the world my debtor !
Or, rather, grant it mine to show
  Such love as once was shown to me,
In days of childhood, long ago,
  Beside my mother's knee !

DEATH AND LIFE

(FROM THE ITALIAN)

FAREWELL, farewell! Aloft on eager wing,
In highest heaven I hear the glad lark sing:
While, thro' the gather'd cloud and mists of night,
Trembles and breaks at last the morning's light.

Far, far afield I hear the heifers low;
(So bounteous, Life, to fill, to overflow?)
A healthful breath mounts from the well-till'd plain. . . .
But me these pleasant scenes may not detain.

To me the richness of the year's last rose
No temperate autumn sunshine shall disclose:
My flesh is wasted . . . On this casement lone
To-morrow's light will break, and find me gone!

GRATITUDE

     No !
   Love is free,
   And scorns like usury.
   Let me then ask for nothing better
   Than to have the world my debtor !
Or, rather, grant it mine to show
  Such love as once was shown to me,
In days of childhood, long ago,
  Beside my mother's knee !

DEATH AND LIFE

(FROM THE ITALIAN)

Farewell, farewell! Aloft on eager wing,
In highest heaven I hear the glad lark sing:
While, thro' the gather'd cloud and mists of night,
Trembles and breaks at last the morning's light.

Far, far afield I hear the heifers low;
(So bounteous, Life, to fill, to overflow?)
A healthful breath mounts from the well-till'd plain. . . .
But me these pleasant scenes may not detain.

To me the richness of the year's last rose
No temperate autumn sunshine shall disclose:
My flesh is wasted . . . On this casement lone
To-morrow's light will break, and find me gone!

NOTES

DEDICATION

'Flowerets of the night.' The Evening Primrose (*Œnothera eximia*), which blooms but for a single evening, perishing at daybreak; and the Night Stock (*Mathiola bicornis*), which, scentless and withered in appearance during the day, revives at night to exhale a ravishing perfume.

The borrowed phrases in the fourth and last lines scarcely require acknowledgment.

THE OMEN, l. 11.

'Carico d' anni e di peccati pieno.'—MICHAEL ANGELO'S *Sonnets*.

THE 'LIGHTNING BEFORE DEATH.'

Reading for the first time through De Quincey's *Confessions*, some years after this poem was first published, I find that the analogy between an 'Indian Summer' and what Shakespeare calls the 'lightning before death' had struck the Opium-Eater many years before it struck myself.

THE WANING YEAR.

'After a fine harvest month, we have had rain almost every day throughout October. The leaves, soaked in moisture, nipped from the trees by frost, or torn off before their time by heavy gales, lie thick and spongy on the earth. I don't remember a year when the melancholy of Autumn has been so apparent, or has affected me so much.'—*Extract from a Journal*.

A Reverie.

> '*The toilworn Pilgrim grey.*'—Monte Pellegrino, near Palermo.

The Nurse's Tale is an experiment in doggerel verse. That this coarse medium is capable, in dexterous hands, of effectively presenting an incident or a character is sufficiently proved by Lord Southesk's poem of *Pigworm and Dixie*, by the *Symon and Janet* of Andrew Scott, the Border Poet, and by the works of Crabbe *passim*. In an age of over-refinement and effeteness in literature, it might perhaps be revived occasionally, not without advantage.

Elegy on an Angler-Poet.

> '*What nights were theirs! how brave a feast!*'

> 'O noctes, cœnæque deûm!' *Noctes* of Horace and of Christopher North.

> '*To others other gifts,*' &c.

> "Ἄλλοις μὲν τεὸν ὄλβον, ἐμοὶ δ' ἀπέλειπες ἀοιδάν.—Moschus, *Idyll* iii. 104.

> '*But thee, we now departing,*' etc.

> 'Ergo in æternum, frater, ave atque vale.'—Catullus, Poem 101.

A Winter Song.

> 'Su 'l viso de l'amore
> La rosa illanguidì,
> Senza lasciarmi un fiore
> La gioventù fuggì.'—Giosuè Carducci.

For the Last Night of the Year.

The Christmas of 1889 was a 'green Yule'—there had been no snow and but little frost. The afternoon of the 31st December was windy; towards twilight the sky became overclouded, and at night rain fell.

DEATH AND LIFE.

The beautiful original of this inadequate translation—beginning with the words, which are a poem in themselves yet poetically untranslatable, 'Muoio, cantan le allodole,'—forms the final page of a volume entitled 'Postuma.' This purports to contain the poetical remains of one Lorenzo Stecchetti, collected by his friend, Olindo Guerrini, of Bologna. A most plausible account of the deceased and of his premature death is prefixed to the book; but the entire volume is now acknowledged to be a fabrication of its gifted but eccentric editor.

www.ingramcontent.com/pod-product-compliance
Lightning Source LLC
Chambersburg PA
CBHW020326090426
42735CB00009B/1417